Math Counts

Children's Press®
An Imprint of Scholastic Inc.

About This Series

In keeping with the major goals of the National Council of Teachers of Mathematics, children will become mathematical problem solvers, learn to communicate mathematically, and learn to reason mathematically by using the series Math Counts.

Pattern, Shape, and *Size* may be investigated first—in any sequence.

Sorting, Counting, and *Numbers* may be used next, followed by *Time, Length, Weight,* and *Capacity.*

—Ramona G. Choos, Professor of Mathematics,
Senior Adviser to the Dean of Continuing Education, Chicago State University;
Sponsor for Chicago Elementary Teachers' Mathematics Club

Author's Note

Mathematics is a part of a child's world. It is not only interpreting numbers or mastering tricks of addition or multiplication. Mathematics is about ideas. These ideas have been developed to explain particular qualities such as size, weight, and height, as well as relationships and comparisons. Yet all too often the important part that an understanding of mathematics will play in a child's development is forgotten or ignored.

Most adults can solve simple mathematical tasks without the need for counters, beads, or fingers. Young children find such abstractions almost impossible to master. They need to see, talk, touch, and experiment.

The photographs and text in these books have been chosen to encourage talk about topics that are essentially mathematical. By talking, the young reader can explore some of the central concepts that support mathematics. It is on an understanding of these concepts that a student's future mastery of mathematics will be built.

—Henry Pluckrose

Math Counts

By Henry Pluckrose

Mathematics Consultant: Ramona G. Choos, Professor of Mathematics

Children's Press®

An Imprint of Scholastic Inc.

SCHOLASTIC

Look at the shape of this page.
Run your fingers around
the edges of the page.
What shape did you trace?

Was it a square, like this?

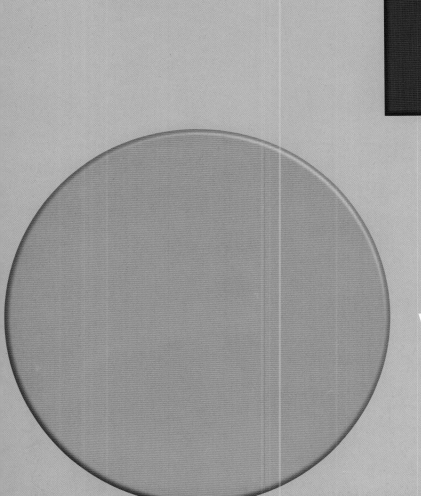

Was it a circle, like this?

Was it a hexagon, like this?

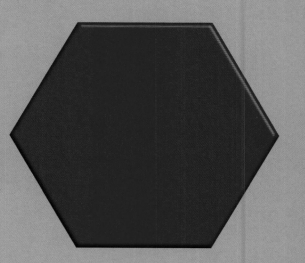

Was it a rectangle, like this?

Was it a triangle, like this?

Squares, circles, hexagons, rectangles, and triangles are regular shapes. Each shape is easy to recognize. What shape can you see here?

In what ways are these
squares similar to one another?
In what ways are they different?

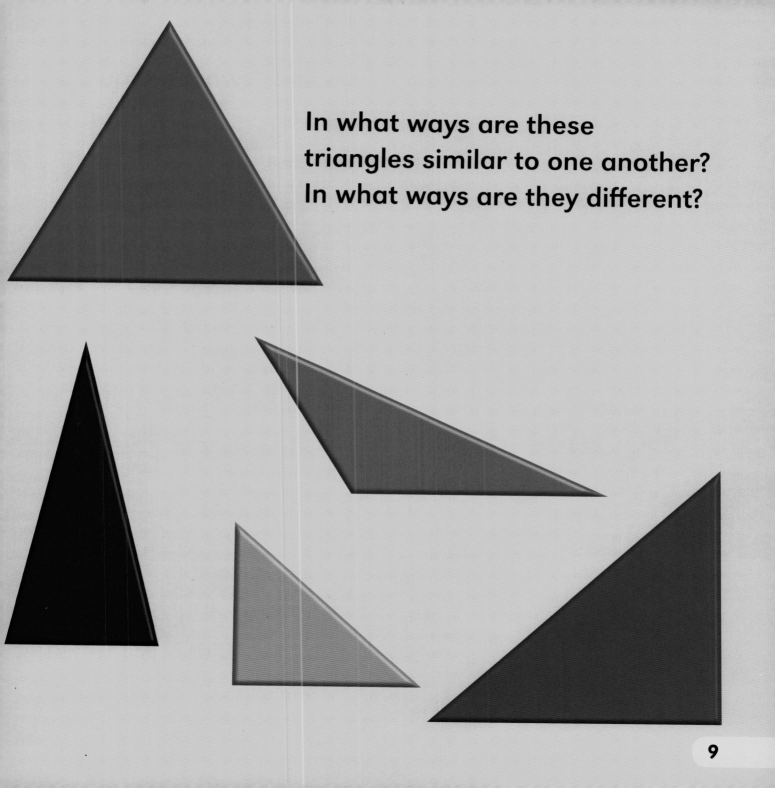

In what ways are these triangles similar to one another? In what ways are they different?

We can find regular shapes almost anywhere—squares,

circles,

rectangles,

and even hexagons.

We can also find regular shapes in nature.
This is a honeycomb made by bees.
Each honeycomb cell has six sides.
Each side is the same length.
Each cell is a hexagon.

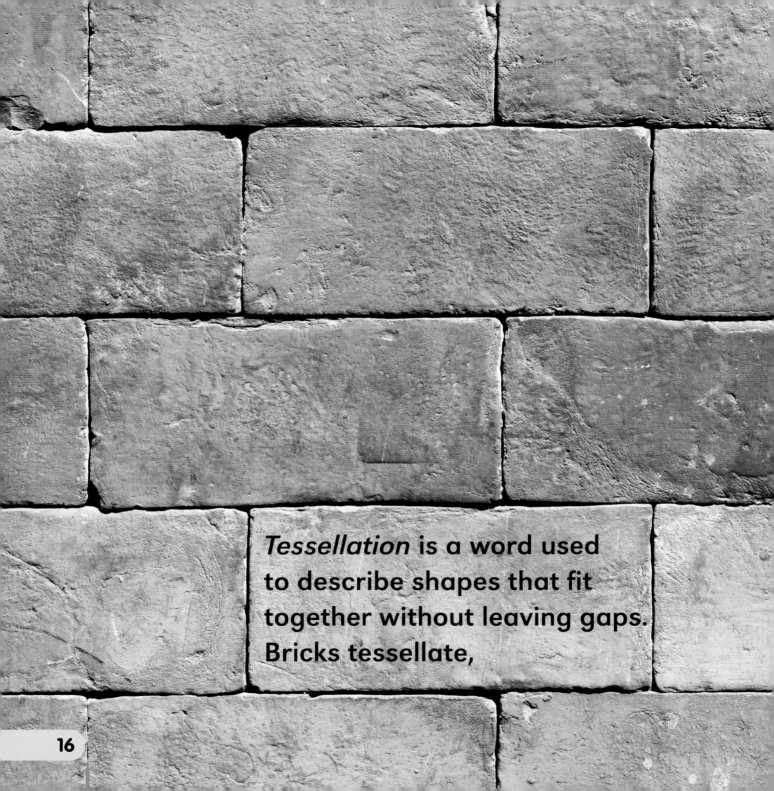

Tessellation is a word used to describe shapes that fit together without leaving gaps. Bricks tessellate,

and so do wooden blocks like these.

You can put some shapes
so close together that they touch.
Do circles tessellate?

Will these triangles
fit together so that no spaces
are left between them?

Sometimes the shape of things seems to change when we look at them from a different angle. What shape are these cans?

These are the same cans.
Now they seem to be a different shape.

What shapes can you recognize here?

What shapes can you see now?

Shapes are used everywhere.
Some are used to give
messages to drivers.
What do these signs mean?

What shapes can
you find in each sign?
Why are some road signs
set in a circle?
Why are others in a triangle?

Many things are shaped for their job.
Why is a clock face round?

Why aren't wheels square?

Look for shapes inside other shapes.
How many regular shapes can you find in this bicycle

and in this steam engine?

Not everything
has a regular shape.
Clouds have ever-changing
shapes, and so do trees
as they sway in the wind.

You have a shape, too, but it is not made up of squares and circles. How is your face different from the face of this clown?

Index

Reader's Guide

Visit this Scholastic Web site to download the Reader's Guide for this series:
www.factsfornow.scholastic.com Enter the keywords **Math Counts**

Library of Congress Cataloging-in-Publication Data
Names: Pluckrose, Henry, 1931– author. | Choos, Ramona G., consultant.
Title: Shape/by Henry Pluckrose; mathematics consultant: Ramona G. Choos, Professor of Mathematics.
Other titles: Math counts.
Description: Updated edition. | New York: Children's Press, an imprint of Scholastic Inc., 2019. | Series: Math counts | Includes index.
Identifiers: LCCN 2017061279| ISBN 9780531175118 (library binding) | ISBN 9780531135204 (pbk.)
Subjects: LCSH: Geometry—Juvenile literature. | Shapes—Juvenile literature.
Classification: LCC QA445.5 .P547 2019 | DDC 516/.15—dc23
LC record available at https://lccn.loc.gov/2017061279

Copyright © The Watts Publishing Group, 2018
Printed in Heshan, China 62

Scholastic Inc., 557 Broadway, New York, NY 10012.

1 2 3 4 5 6 7 8 9 10 R 28 27 26 25 24 23 22 21 20 19

Photos ©: 7: Masaki Kai/EyeEm/Getty Images; 10: Jake Fitzjones/Getty Images; 11: Ball Songwut/Shutterstock; 12: Dougall_Photography/iStockphoto; 13: Michael Rosskothen/Shutterstock; 14: Melvica Amor Omictin/EyeEm/Getty Images; 15: StudioSmart/Shutterstock; 16: Celig/Shutterstock; 17: assalve/iStockphoto; 18: Andrii Medvednikov/Shutterstock; 20: Bernard Van Berg/EyeEm/Getty Images; 21: MarioGuti/iStockphoto; 22: Sumikophoto/Dreamstime; 23: Karol Franks/Getty Images; 24 top left: Christian Delbert/Shutterstock; 24 top right: Lindasj22/Shutterstock; 24 bottom: Lester Balajadia/Shutterstock; 25 top: Carlos E. Santa Maria/Shutterstock; 25 bottom left: njnightsky/iStockphoto; 25 bottom right: artcphotos/Shutterstock; 26: knoppper/iStockphoto; 27: s_oleg/Shutterstock; 28: Andrew Bonnenfant/EyeEm/Getty Images; 29: Kent Kobersteen/Getty Images; 30: Alexander Rieber/EyeEm/Getty Images; 31: Andreas Gradin/Shutterstock.